F Scott and J,

Turn

with thanks

and

WENDY
CHIN-TANNER

gratitude,

Sibling Rivalry Press
Alexander, Arkansas
www.SiblingRivalryPress.com

Literary Arts, 4/2/15

Sibling Rivalry Press, LLC
13913 Magnolia Glen Drive
Alexander, AR 72002

info@siblingrivalrypress.com

www.siblingrivalrypress.com

ISBN: 978-1-937420-60-4

Library of Congress Control Number: 2013956732

First Sibling Rivalry Press Edition, March 2014

For my grandmother,
Shuet King Kwok (1925-2010)

TURN

I

II

TURN

III

I.

1

On the beach where they played the shell game, my eyes
looked out to sea.

Walking, forgetful of last steps over broken sand,
I wished then

to know nothing, wanting only to fuse
with the fog rolling in, to reach

the city of light shining, surely,
over the horizon.

TEMPEST

1.

Before the rain, the river
sweeps its gusty air down the street
from the Promenade. A cloud of dust
gathers over her halo of permed hair.

2.

She is sweeping the front stoop of the Dutch House
with crablike steps, short legs bowed from the births
of seven children, and I,
the only daughter of the second unwanted girl,
watch the passing cars splash the puddle
always lingering at the curb, waiting
beneath the umbrella of the Brooklyn tree
for the first cool drops to fall.

3.

One morning, there is a fuss: Mother
beats my legs with the bamboo handle
of the feather duster and I run.
She follows me, silently waving Mother away,
and soothes me with the smell of her,
of Tiger Balm and something acid
and female underneath.

4.

My wet cheek slipping against the back
of her silky floral shirt, she hoists me into the mei tai
she made me from scraps left over from the factory,
though I am already too big and she'd urged Mother
to do it for my own good, she says, so
I would not become a monster.

5.

I am her creature. Her
Caliban. Or am I Miranda
with my thin winter skin? Mother
says I am the child of milk, eggs,
and avoiding dark foods
during pregnancy.

6.

It has been years since I have passed through
those squealing gates but every stain,
every scar inflicted on the surface of that house
finds itself at home within me:
the rot on the kitchen floorboards;
the soiled splotches on the velvet couch;
the barren garden leveled by a storm;
and the boxes stacked up to the chandeliers
throughout that once majestic space, making a maze.

7.

It's easier to remember these details—to no longer
feel the night gaping outside the window,
the yawning maw waiting to swallow me whole.
The scenes of my memory have, like
celluloid, unreeled, melted into dreams.

8.

It's easier to forget the Saturday in November,
the bag of apples in front of the TV showing *Fist of Fury*,
with him using Grandfather's knife to turn the skins of each
bright fruit into single red strands before biting
into their floury white flesh, bite after bite, eating
one after the next insatiably, and me, hands clutching
my own apple, trying not to let my eyes stray from the screen.

9.

In my own bedroom at home with Father,
a dresser drawer drops onto my foot
and even before the shooting pain comes,
the big toenail turns a deep purple-black,
but I stifle the howl, afraid of Father's
anxious anger and gingerly pull on my pink knee-socks.

10.

I do not ask for Mother. Instead, I call for her
as I did when, delirious with chicken pox,
the late-summer rain had turned to hail,
and that transformation of the soft drops
into hard frozen pebbles became forever
tangled in my mind with the marks on my face.

11.

I beg then to be taken to the Dutch House where
in the kitchen, I show her what I have done.
She speaks gently, then mixes a poultice, Prospero
grinding dried medicinal bees together
with a foul-smelling herb steeped in bitter wine.

12.

She holds Grandfather's lighter under a fat sewing needle
until its sharp silver point glows orange and blue.
She pierces the shell of my ruined toe.
It releases the pressure so that magically
the blackened blood oozes out a cheerful red.
She covers the drained wound with cotton and gauze.

13.

She promises in a quiet voice that this will be our secret.

IN THE DUTCH HOUSE

If here, where
the blare of the television hid
nothing and the eyes
of the bloated goldfish
were glazed with rheum,

I told you
that my bearing was filial,
compassionate, and kind,
it would be a lie.

Cigarette burns peppered the carpets.
Each day we put out small fires,
put away sharp things
after he came at her once with a pair of scissors,
lurching forward on his cane and his spindly legs.

What kind of man was this?

He beat his wife and sometimes his children.
He was fond of babies and teasing.
He fought the dogs his sons raised as pets.
He saved from the Communists a collection of rare scrolls.

He would not speak of the madness that struck his favorite son,
but insisted that evil spirits were hiding in the walls.
Though he read the classics,
he pissed on the toilet seat and shat his pants.
He raged. He shook his penis in the hallway.
She would bathe him then with damp rags

as he wept with his bald head bowed.
The liver spots clotted into continents and
she was pleased with his wretchedness.
She loved him.
She finally had him.
She knew he could never leave her.

In the garden with him
the autumn before the end began,
I raked the leaves that fell from the tall oak tree
and despite the neighbors' warnings,
he burned them in the tin tofu bin
along with the spirit money and joss papers.

Beneath a cluster of leaves,
I overturned a pigeon's corpse,
flattened, already decomposing.

I thought that we might bury it,
but he threw it onto the illegal fire
and the stench of the smoldering, putrid feathers
drove me indoors,
nostrils and eyelids burning,
as the thick black smoke curled
up—beyond
the Brooklyn sky.

I CANNOT SAY

I cannot say what
was said or
what was touched or
how long it went on.
I cannot say.

When they took me home
after the long work day, I could no longer
be with them in the same way.

When he hurled that cheap
vase across the room,
he could not say
why.

She could not say why
she ricocheted
like shards of china
shattering against the wall.

I thought that if I could find the right words,
they would hold us together,

but there were no words.
How could I tell his stories,
the porn stacked inside
the broken fridge,
the things that happened to girls?

FABLES

I.

O Little Sparrow, so tender and so
young, feeding on the worms and grubs

that your mama brung.
She doesn't rest, carrying them

squirming to the nest.
But as soon as you're hatched, you leave,

flying up above the eaves, chirping and
cheeping merrily while your mama weeps.

2.

O Little Firefly, it's late and the evening's
losing its light. What are you coming for?

For your midnight oil. What will you
hold it in? Hold it in a porcelain bowl

painted with blossoms of silver and
gold, though the bowl has been scratched by

a grain of fine sand. See that great
man astride his white horse? This child

rides a winter melon and still he gets bucked
down to the ground. But when he falls, he

plucks a flower. Child, give Grandmother what
you have found, though she might think it far

too red. So give it to your Grandpa instead, and
he will slay a chicken and play

the Drumsong. Beat the drums loudly! Beat the
Warlord! For his line has grown so horribly long.

3.

O Sister Jade, marrying Mr. Lee,
he's punting across the lake to claim you

with a basketful of chicken legs and a
basketful of cake—enough for your mother-

in-law, a little for yourself, and some to serve your
husband—smile! Such luck and so much wealth!

4.

Everything yields its place and goes,
Sister Winter, Pure Snow.

The child you named the Instrument
of Grace, whose body was made

within your brine, whose face
they said would never shine, whose

thoughts you carved with sharpened
words, became a woman

draped in silk and furs. She broke
the mirror, but in her eye, a splinter

of glass had flown inside. Then what
she had wanted to be, she wanted me

to be: a china doll; a queen
bee; a perfect plot; her proxy.

MAGNOLIA (HUA MULAN)

Dear Mother, can you remember how
that spring was the first time I joined the women

shearing the goats and sheep, boiling
their raw wool to dye and weave into blood

red cloth? Finally tall enough to reach,
I stretched them to dry on tenterhooks.

I saw in your eyes that you were proud.
On the horizon in the tenter-fields,

a sea of women swam, their colored flaps taut
like sails in the breeze. One day, they parted

for the Imperial Army. The Huns and Turks
had spilled, they said, across our western border.

No family was exempt from duty,
but Father was too old, so you gave me

Baby Brother's clothes and told me to go.
That night, the warm air turned suddenly raw.

We shut the windows and the wind wept
because we would not let it in.

In the thin dark before morning, we whispered
goodbye. The shutters were closed and I was glad

our house could not see me go. Riding
west, there was nothing but soldiers marching,

an army of ants in the undulant grass
moving forward relentlessly

under the perfectly curved sky. My horse walked
in the exact center of the dome heading west.

Though we were near the edge of the Kingdom,
I could not get out of the middle

of that circle. Surely the gods had blessed
me, for mile after mile though the sun began

to set, the circle still surrounded me
protectively, unchanging. All around the edge

of the land, the air blushed pink
as peonies. I watched the colors slowly

drain from everything with each step
as the shadows of our horses grew

into giant beasts and the horizon sank
into a clear pale gray. Thickly above us,

the night seemed to glitter with strings
of pearls and the yellow moon beamed so full

of light that the stars squinted and barely blinked.
The men, sharing strong drink, sang the ballad

of the Lady in the Moon who had only
her rabbit for a friend. As I fell asleep

in the camp that night, the sound of their voices
grew sweet and reedy and far away, and

in my sleep, I dreamt that it was your voice singing.
In the morning, the prairie loomed too large

and the winds streaked through the grass shrieking
dark thoughts. From the south, great black clouds

billowed up, stripping the rays away
from the sun as if it were setting again.

A horde of rabbits bounded past,
in a panic between the horses' legs

as if we were merely an army of
terracotta men. Behind them, fire

came screaming as thousands of birds flew
across the plains. We galloped, maintaining

our line over the western edge of the world,
the fire pushing us towards the enemy.

We were hemmed in. We could neither
halt nor retreat, and so it was done.

Nothing was left for us but war. After
thirteen years, I am a woman now.

But on the field, I was the fiercest of men.
With my comrades, I bled. I led them

against the swords and arrows of legions.
bloodying and conquering ten thousand

women's sons. But I'm finished now. Wounded
by barbarians, I was stripped and found out.

In my disgrace, my manhood has been replaced
with celebrity. The Son of Heaven himself

knighted me Xiaolie, Hero of Filial
Piety, and with this title,

I was to become his concubine. I replied,
I have earned my rank as General, Sir,

not Wife. And so, dishonored and discharged,
I am coming home. I long to tear off

my military robes and slip on my red silk gown.
If I close my eyes, I can feel

your comb running its teeth through my hair,
your fingertips sweeping my bare temples.

Leaning against the lintel, I will die,
watching the willows dip into our pond.

Out the window, I will welcome the night
arriving with all her familiar stars.

JOAN

Perhaps uncertain of God's grace,
in her own shaky, illiterate
hand, she signed Jehanne

before burning for the crime
of crossdressing. Her eyes
fixed on the cross, dying,
the coals were raked back
from the stake to expose her

blackened body, to make
no mistake, and then she burned again
to ash to leave no relic.

No feminist, in the name of
the Lord, she let no women
soldier and slapped the whores
with the flat of her sword.

When the executioner confessed
he was afraid to be damned, she prayed
to God that he be saved
as he set her ablaze.

PERSEPHONE

Stem of my heart, sharp end of my
    anchor, Mother, creator, drunkard

at the revels of your endless spring, your face
    was turned—you did not see Death take

my hand and twirl me down into
    the belly of the earth. I have not seen

your winters, when, inconsolable, you
    blight the fields, pelt them with snow, punish

because I slipped from your grip.
    After, I never remember how it was

with him, what we did in our season
    below. In my mind I can see the black river,

the cold blue chamber. There was a mirror
    and the girl within it is no longer a child.

I hate her, I would choke her dead, I
    would drive her off, but she cleaves

to me, despicable stillborn twin.
    For your sake, I pretend that I am she.

On my return, the budding trees also pretend
    that life can be renewed again as before, as if

after the harvest the fields would not fallow
          and your ripened fruits would never fall. As if he

has released me forever and I am free
          to love another. Tell me, Mother, if

his stench did not make things grow, would
          you have saved me from Death, your brother?

MOTHER

Even before I had begun to menstruate,
Mother bought a box of junior tampons
so that I would not miss my ballet class
when the bleeding came.

In the rose-tiled bathroom
I was to practice
inserting and extricating them.

Mother clutched the pink diagram,
a miniature woman cross-sectioned,
as she watched my performance
and then tried to help me maneuver
the dry wad into my imperforate insides.

She had not been so intimate with my body
for more than a decade when,
after prompting me on the toilet, she would wipe my
vagina, calling it little toad in Toisanese.

When I was giving birth, I did not want her
at the labor; I did not want her
to see my nakedness
or the sudden surge and downward shrug
of one body emerging from another.

And afterwards I did not want her
to see me slack-bellied, bleeding week
upon week into the coarse cotton pads,

so like the ones she had used years before;
foam bricks rolled up and discarded,
rotting each month in the garbage can
full of bitterness.

FATHER

Already I can hear him, the defiant
slip-slap of his flip-flops on my narrow steps,
a jack-in-the-box recoiling
and springing back relentlessly
against the hand that pushes.

I can see us as we were long ago at the piano,
framed in the tableau of the doorway to the old living room:

the little girl and the father,
her hand pushing away,
his not quite slapping back.

I never wanted to listen to the looping
reportage, the endless retellings boyishly
chasing one disaster after another, fables
marching into my memory,
soldiers glimpsed through the blanket
of leaves he hid under in the roadside ditch.

My ears refused to
translate his messages:

why his mother's hand had clamped so tightly over his mouth
that day, how he lost her and then, sailing across the sea, slept
on a cold cot at the back of the laundromat in the Bronx
until with the diagnosis he came to pass a long ellipsis
interned in the Southern sanitarium.

Tracing scars, my fingers tried to read
the patterns in the tracks running up his arms
and into the sleeves of his cotton undershirts, sensing,
as he spoke, in my own body the smell
and struggle of twilight sleep.

He should be sleeping now, suspended
between the earth and the dawn, gliding
eastward over the water, over Greenland
and Ireland and England, almost

old, the years in their irreducible procession
filing onward through their dwindling supply,
his temples showing only a dusting of white;

snow freshly fallen onto soil.

PERSIMMONS ON SUNDAY

In the kitchen, I smell the pungent perfume
of persimmons overripe in the sun,
imagine their burnt orange bodies
quartered into jeweled wedges
on a good china plate.

In the palm of my left hand, I hold
the gelatinous speckled fruit
as I have seen my mother do
while in my right the knife
I'm not supposed to touch
glides through the flesh,
so fast that it slices without thought
into my four extended fingertips.

I'm watching this happen:
the alizarin streams;
the viscous juices
trickling down from wrist to elbow;
the red riven from the orange;

a curious astonishment
before the sting.

NO MOON

In the old beige station wagon straining forward
on the road like a dog
frantically sniffing for the way home,

we are lost in the winding countryside, overgrown
branches scratching the roof
as the signs bearing route numbers grow
too dark to read after a day spent hunting property;

a house, some land, some water
where we could run, a precaution after Chernobyl
when we drank only powdered milk and frozen juice for a year.

In the front seat, Ma and Ba sit
silhouetted in silence, sustained in the green glow
of the dashboard, a play
of shadows flitting from the landscape over their faces.

Across the broad lap of the leather backseat, I lie
supine as the daylight that had earlier been
so dazzling and bright dancing
in the paisley of the real estate agent's scarf

fades from dusk to a black
whose dense immensity, though the opposite
of light, holds its own kind of clarity,
a reminder of how far

you could fall, and I imagine that the car door

could suddenly unlatch and I would fly
out into that darkness, into the woods, into the universe.
Outside my window above the blur,
I scan the horizon for a still spot,

but a shooting star screeches, skidding
across the night and amid the clouds tumbling
thick and ink-smeared and round,

there is no moon to be found until long after we arrive
when its battered face appears,

a pale ghost hanging in the morning sky.

SHAME

I did not swallow
but held it
folded like a secret
in my mouth.

2

I had fallen in love with the water
and after years of fighting

its rough salty waves, I was washed ashore,
raving, tumbling

over and over myself like sea glass,
head over ass.

I COULD NOT FORGIVE YOU

For walking under the same sky
and sleeping on the same earth
those days and nights,

I could not forget it

even when we lay down
and the rain sank into our pores and my belly

rose up and up like a cloud.

I have awoken
from a long, dark sleep.

What place was it? What time?

You were looking forward;
I tried not to look behind.

BOTANY

These saplings we have bedded
     side by side
         that winnow unseeing roots
             through the exhaling loam,
                that drink with pale reaching
          tendrils from wellsprings
        wending, whorling crystalline
      underground, grow out from
their cringing pods and
     uncurl their coiled heads, stretching
        arms and fingers,
          untwining,
             the linden
             from the oak,
        to straighten
      together, I think,
    towards the same
naked light.

WINTER

I dared you to tell me what you could not
say and you did, then, fecund, fucking

madly behind drawn blinds, there was no day
or night in the noisy bed. Ever contrary, you

were in the frigid air a poinsettia blooming,
simple and naked, big body laid atop

sheets, heat broken. It was winter.
The short days lent themselves to talk,

and frozen, the river paddled by night stood
erect in peaks of ice. The afternoons

grew longer and the river ran again, the water
rushing, my waters quickening unplanned.

FREE

Pregnant,

skin thin as wet rice paper,
tense membrane
separating
water from water,
body from body.
The bottom spills
suddenly
out from the pail.

The absence
remains in my hands.

VETERAN

Maybe it's because I returned from that
ruinless war victorious by

surrendering, having given over
to myself as some do to God,

conquistadora of mind and pain so
that the day was mine, as the blood I shed,

gushing freely down my thighs onto the
bed, as the child delivered to us by

assiduous suffering. Remember,
in those Sisyphean hours, how nearly

her dark head crowned again and again, and
then slipped back behind the lip of labor's

end, 'til the midwives suggested mildly
that we should perhaps go, but I said no,

and you took me at my word. I was in
between places, at once within and with-

out, arms outstretched as I stood, legs apart,
touching one wall and the other, possessed.

When our bodies parted, it was without
violence. She slid from me like a sloop

on the crest of that final mighty wave,
the surge sucking her backwards before

spilling over, like breath, like confession,
her arms reaching forward towards the dry

open shore and mine reaching down
to receive her, meet her, round bright

bud of us combined, her astonishing
glaucous eyes staring steadily,

curiously, seeming to see. It's because
of this, I think, that later we became

so hungry for each other. Even with
the bleeding and leaking, I was shining

in your eyes like a fairy queen, and I
too was changed, so that when I came that first

time after the birth, the hot pink lily
that was left and buried in the dirt

unfurled as we fucked, such hunger, such thirst.
Our hips bucked, and the confetti from your

cock burst, a shower, a tickertape parade
celebrating inside, discreetly crying

out victory, rising so high above
you and me and everything we knew.

HIDE AND SEEK

sun moon truth
come out
come out
wherever you are

THROUGH THE BATHROOM DOOR

I hear my husband and our little girl
above the tempest in my head.
I cannot drown their voices singing
about ducks and fish and washing.

Those first months, it was her insistent cries
for milk and the tender gush that would
release me from the squall-

ing. Breasts
filling and draining to the rhythm of
her clucking chin, my mind
would wash clean
as her drunken eyes fluttered closed.

I have told myself the story of
my life in ten thousand conflicting tales;
I have pored over them with a jeweler's
loupe for true stones,
meanings, and despite such careful study,

nothing could hold back
the surge once the swell had broken.

I had wanted to lie next to them
as if they held the answers
in their four open hands,
as if my vigilance could keep us safe,
as if language and names and places
could be clean.

MIND AND WILL

The monkey on the horse's back
careering in full gallop across the boundless fallow fields

lets the reins fall
by the edge of the clearest silver mere.

What brings them to halt
but the willingness to drink?

RAIN

When the midday darkens
and the low rumble of distant thunder
descends, we rush to the balcony in bathing suits
to wait for the storm.

Jumping up and down as the first drops
fall big as blueberries from the clouds,
she tilts back her head
to catch them in her open mouth,
jaws a widely spread hinge.

She touches our wet cheeks
with the palms of her hands,
traces rivers from
our noses to our chins.

We are not afraid
even when the lightning strikes
so close that the concrete
quivers beneath our feet;
we are stomping
and singing
a nonsense song.

We are dancing,

we are shivering,
in the August rain.

III.

3

My pockets are empty.
I have let go of all I have known

to stand here, to look both ways
before crossing.

HARVEST MOON

After the midnight feeding, breath sweet
and easy with milk,

Maddy curls into a comma, a crescent moon
still in the night.

While slowly letting go, I creep
across the cool floorboards back to the big bed.

Tyler holds the duvet open as, pressing
against the warm bowl of his stomach, I remember

my mother's sachets of rice wrapped hot
in clean white handkerchiefs, how she rolled the steaming
bundles

redolent with jasmine
over my bellyaches, the comfort

of that yielding heat. Turning my ear to him,
I hear the murmur of his resting heart.

And beyond us, faceless, floating in the night,
the moon burns through the window,

an unclosing eye.

SAYING YES

Though they said that you would,
you do not forget the pain

of your sacrum and pubic bone yawning wide
open like a rusted gate that could not close,
and, when she was flopped onto your breast,
of her face unfurling before you like a fist
as the grip on the bird fluttering in your chest let go.

Grasping both your hands,
she scales your body
like a monument,
heels digging into the fasciae of your thighs,
feet perching square on each of your hips,

and you imagine that you could sail
up like balloons over what had ruined you,
the wrong beginnings, the wrong turns;

you wonder if after all you haven't missed your chance
when, poking her snub nose into yours,
she fixes you with your own familiar gaze,

and asks, *Mama? Are you happy?*
her voice lifting up so high,

Mama? You say yes?

GENJOKOAN

Too late
in its fall,
it had tried to fly.
Oh no! No!
No! Madeleine cries.
And then,
too late,
I try to lie.

Ladybugs can't swim,

Mama! She demands,
You have to fix him!

Out in the garden,

the sky
rests

while the moon
in a pool
darkened by night

stays dry, unhindered,

and the water
sits still, unburdened,

unbroken by light.

RABBIT

Maddy is coughing, coughing, breath catching
in her chest, crying, arms up in the air, calling
Mama into the darkness that lies

between us and in seconds, as if she
were weightless, damp heat
draped over my shoulder, I am rocking,

humming with my eyes closed, seeing

myself again as I was in the old house kneeling
at the foot of the bed those sleepless nights, playing
the game with my rabbit

in the secret circle of light, how

I slapped her again and again to the rose-carpeted floor, then
hugged her quickly back to my breast, petting
her, consoling her, warmth rising in my chest.

BIND

Last night, you asked for my milk and I
said no, though you cried

and whined. My breasts ache
and I have no cloths to bind

them. It's time.

Instead, I rocked you and
stroked your spine until you
shuddered and laid still, a foal,
limbs folded, in my lap.

And we stayed like that,
me holding you,
whispering nursery rhymes,

a pieta, but, breasts weeping,
the stigmata was mine.

WHEN YOU OPEN IT TO SPEAK

Has it been four years already since you
were pushed from my womb, a thrashing fish
slicked with blood, heart throbbing, a Valentine

in my hands? While brushing my teeth, I hear
you joke in bed with your dad, giggling
that you had come out of his head.

And remembering how in my fourth grade book
Athena had leapt from Zeus' crown as the axe
split him open, her lips parted, pealing

to the broad blue sky, a daughter fully grown
and armed, and her father clutching at
his labor pains, I think how wise

you are, as you did emerge with a cry
as much from your father's imagination as from
your mother's ache.

FIFTH

Over this handspan of years,
my reflection
has been caught
in your bedside mirror,
sharp or dull
depending on the hour,
the light, the season,
how long I look.

Funny how the eye
can only see itself this way.

The first year,
we were like paper,
tearable yet unwritten.

Here. Take

this unadorned body,
this uncarved block.

We should burn
like wood,
like a good bonfire,
leaving no trace.

ON THE THAMESPATH

Between brambles and brushwood, meadowsweet
and quaking grass, we are no longer as

we were that winter, breath smoking, trailing
white ghosts under clouds hanging heavy-

bellied with sleet that would fall, then freeze and
thaw later in our sleep. But there in a

brief flood of pale western light, you stopped and
held your hand in mine, standing before the

hours, the days succeeding nights, week upon
week, bending us through the years. The thornbush

in our path has spent its blossom for
berry. And the river beneath its sea

of silent glass seethes in black currents and
eddies. The steady live rush carries on.

IN THE BEST POSSIBLE OUTCOME

I will bury you or you
will bury me and we will

have loved as if
tomorrow had already gone.

SIGNS AND SYMBOLS
For KSK (1957-2009)

These last weeks, I've been searching for signs—
on the Hudson a red helicopter hovering above a boat

called Quantum while across from Liberty the faces
of the clocktower stand frozen at five past four, first

at the deli, then at the café, "Proud Mary" playing.
And out my bedroom window, the strange bright chirps

of the birds building a nest in the blind winter night.
And, speaking of birds, everywhere the pigeons that have

been flying at me—one scrabbling its claws against my umbrella,
another glancing off the top of my wool hat, though homely

and dirty, its wings outstretched with confidence—
since you fell from the sky. Once you were a small boy

who didn't cry when you were stung by a bee, but accused
with dry eyes, *Look! Look! Now, I told you it would bite!*

Then it was you who called me Tough Guy in Toisanese
when I had stifled my tears after grazing my knees,

and then held me, my chubby arms slung around your neck.
Later, you told me how matter could be neither created

nor destroyed, and, since the universe was breathing, expanding
and contracting like sand dissolving into the sea,

it was possible for particles to behave as waves,
waves as particles, joined in space and time.

WAKE

He speaks to me
as if to a stranger,
thanking me for coming.

The monks are chanting

and I nod
repetitively,
unhearing

like the drinking bird perched
on the edge of his glass,

not a real bird,

just a pair of bulbs
joined by a reed-thin tube
bobbing rhythmically

that cartoon head,
that motion nothing
but a function
of the pressure within.

CHRISTMAS PRESENT

I want to be happy,
I want to forget,
my mother says, reading my poem
for her brother who is dead.

I ask, *Why?* and she starts to cry.
Then my father barks, his voice climbing high,

You go too far!
And you keep going on!
Blah! Blah! Blah! he says I say.

You're just like me. We're the same way.
We don't care, I hear my daddy say,
what anyone feels, you see.
Not like her —
she wears her heart on her sleeve.
But you…

Well, what else could I do?

I'm sorry, I say, handing her a tissue,
I still need a mother. I still need you.

And she spits:
I do too!

ALZHEIMER'S

as if childhood had not
died as
if the intervening
years had
not passed you by
giggling she
is peeking at
you through
the widening
lacuna signaling ship
to shore unmoored
but restored to
your own private
time her face the
face of your waking
hours mother's
milk gone
sour if you let it
be again
as it was between
you then what
would happen to
what happened
to what was
real or
true what
would you do?

IN OUR TONGUE

Beginning
with our ugliest dipthong—
th—

we hawk
and splutter
the sound,

singing
th—ee!

greeting death
by name.

O, brutal song.

LITTLE DEATH

Grandma, your tongue twists, making half-joined
sounds. Your good hand points to the bandages, asking

why and when we will go. The nurses studiously
avoid your eyes, accustomed in their way to such

little scenes; another day, another little death.
The summer I learned to read, I asked you the questions

for the citizenship test. We rehearsed them
over and over again: *Are you a Communist?*

No! you'd cry and I'd nod yes, smiling but afraid you might
not pass until finally, standing before the judge, you pledged

your allegiance, hand over heart. Your skin is soft and
plump like a girl's, swollen from the IV, liver spots scattered

sweetly like Brown-eyed Susans in a field
of bruises. I massage your insteps, running

my thumbs again and again over
your warm little feet. In my hands,

they fit perfectly, arching and curling, toenails like pearls
clipped into miniature half moons. Each visit, we do this

and then I leave. At home, with strong soap, I scrub
my hands clean. And I lead my husband to the bedroom.

KEEPSAKE

The pin I took when you were
asleep, slipped in my pocket while

the EEG made your limp limbs
leap. After I flutted your hair back up and said

goodbye, I put it in a pillowed box;

I'll keep it there under all
the junk inside the kitchen drawer,

the rubber bands and string, a strand
of hair still twined in its plastic ruby vine.

THE WHEEL

We fought the summer before
I became a sophomore.

You slammed the drawer and
I closed the door.

And when you shouted from the stoop
as I swooped into the subway,

I didn't know that we would wait
a decade to break the silence we made

impossible to betray.

The incense burns before
the effigies —cardboard cars, spirit

money—minor deities, the family tree
blackening in the urn. The wheel

turns and we love again
not in spite of death but because.

GRATITUDE

I would like to thank Veronica and Mark Davidov, Elizabeth Onusko, Beth Bosworth, Eduardo C. Corral, Garrett Hongo, Nancy White, and all my other friends and teachers who helped bring this book into being.

Thanks to my publisher, Bryan Borland and Eric Thomas Norris, my tireless editor, collaborator, and brother from another mother and another father.

Thanks to my parents, Kam and Walter Chin for giving me their blessing to tell these stories.

And thanks to Tyler and Maddy Chin-Tanner, my muses, my touchstones, my true loves.

ACKNOWLEDGMENTS

Grateful acknowledgment is made to the following publications where these poems or earlier versions first appeared:

The Saint Ann's Review: "In the Dutch House," "Rabbit," "When You Open It to Speak," and "Keepsake"

The Nervous Breakdown: "Shame," "Fifth," and "Harvest Moon," "Veteran"

The Raintown Review: "Bind" and "Genjokoan"

Umbrella: "On the Thamespath"

Stealing Time Magazine: "Saying Yes"

Praxilla: "Wake"

The Lantern Review: "In Our Tongue"

Mascara Literary Review: "No Moon" and "Little Death"

Poetry Pacific: "1," "2," "3," "Free," "Hide and Seek," and "In the Best Possible Outcome."

Softblow: "Mind and Will"

Unshod Quills: "Signs and Symbols"

Forgetting Home: Poems about Alzheimer's (Barefoot Muse Press, 2013): "Alzheimer's"

ABOUT THE POET

Wendy Chin-Tanner's poems, essays, and interviews have appeared in numerous journals including *The Mays Anthology of Oxford and Cambridge*, *The Saint Ann's Review*, and *The Raintown Review*. She is a founding editor at *Kin Poetry Journal* (wearekin.org), poetry editor at *The Nervous Breakdown*, staff interviewer at *Lantern Review*, co-founder of A Wave Blue World (publisher of graphic novels), and an online sociology instructor at Cambridge University, UK. Wendy lives in Portland, Oregon.

ABOUT THE PUBLISHER

Founded in 2010, Sibling Rivalry Press is an independent publishing house based in Alexander, Arkansas. Our mission is to publish work that disturbs and enraptures.

CPSIA information can be obtained at www.ICGtesting.com
Printed in the USA
LVOW11s2113070214

372857LV00001B/2/P

9 781937 420604